Before It's Too Late, Climate

Dean Khater

Copyright © 2023

All Rights Reserved

Dedication

To my wife and my children...

And,

To those who tried and those who are still trying to find solutions and ideas to help humanity and save our planet Earth...

Acknowledgment

This book is based on two-year-long research conducted on climate change which is becoming a serious problem for almost every country in the world.

With all solutions and ideas available nowadays, we still can't stop the effects of climate change; thus, we still need a more practical approach to make the Earth a better place to live in.

I spent hours reading and studying about climate change problems and available solutions. Therefore, finally, I came up with that simple and applicable *"moving seawater inland."*

This is a unique solution the world never heard or thought about before. I believe that solution will bring drastic changes once we implement it to climate change problems.

I acknowledge that this solution can't be implemented without the cooperation between all countries, large conglomerates, and all climate-related world organizations.

Before implementing the solution, professionals are required to study several research papers thoroughly in order to understand its impact on the environment. After going through this phase, we can move seawater inland.

About the Author

Dean Khater is a long-time publisher and researcher in many areas, from IT to Political and Environmental Studies. He graduated from a reputable law school but never practiced law.

Dean used to own computer and software publications for about twenty years. Recently, he started studying climate change to find the core cause and solution. After years of studying, Dean decided to share some of the solutions he learned by publishing his first book, *Before It's Too Late, Climate*.

Currently, Dean is working on a series of books on different genres. He will soon publish books based on fiction stories, true stories, new jokes, and more.

Getting into the great world of writing books after many years of reading and studying is an inspiring experience that he wanted to share with the World.

Contents

DEDICATION I

ACKNOWLEDGMENT II

ABOUT THE AUTHOR III

CONTENTS 4

CHAPTER ONE — INTRODUCTION 1

CHAPTER TWO — WHAT IS CLIMATE CHANGE? 8

CHAPTER THREE — THE PROBLEM WITH CLIMATE CHANGE 18

CHAPTER FOUR — NEW SOLUTION 30

CHAPTER FIVE — EXECUTION 38

CHAPTER SIX — CONCLUSION 44

CHAPTER SEVEN — SUMMARY 51

Chapter One — Introduction

"Countries and cities could be underwater by 2050."

"New data raises concerns over global sea level."

"A new study into how quickly ice sheets melted at the end of the last ice age is raising the alarm over how quickly sea levels could rise in today's warming world."

"UN calls for complete shutdown to fossil fuel shutdown."

"We're running out of time — Climate change is getting BAD."

"Climate change is speeding toward catastrophe. The next decade is crucial, UN Panel says."

"A new report says, 'It is still possible to hold global warming to relatively safe levels, but doing so will require global cooperation, billions of dollars, and big changes.'"

"Scientists deliver 'final warning' on climate crisis: act now or it's too late."

Haven't you read or listened to such news? Aren't you tired of listening to the alarming news of the worsening climate? Won't such news make you think about what will happen in the coming years?

From our computers to phone screens, from our social media feeds to Chrome pages, there is always one post or story about floods, earthquakes, and other calamities, giving us a hint that we are in danger because of changing weather, resulting in more floods, melting of glaciers and awful changes. Some people may say it is not an issue, but it is! Climate Change is real, and it's not to be taken lightly.

Climate change refers to long-term shifts in temperatures and weather patterns. These shifts may be natural, such as through variations in the solar cycle. But since the 1800s, human activities have been the main driver of climate change, primarily due to burning fossil fuels like coal, oil, and gas.

Burning fossil fuels generates greenhouse gas which acts like a blanket wrapped around the Earth, trapping the sun's heat and eventually increasing the global temperature.

Examples of greenhouse gas emissions causing climate change include carbon dioxide and methane, generated from using gasoline for driving a car, or coal electricity for heating a building usually. Moreover, removing grass and green areas from forests and lands is the biggest cause of the increase in carbon dioxide levels across the world. At the same time, garbage is a major source of methane emissions, while industries, transport, buildings, agriculture, and land use are among the main emitters of harmful gases.

Climate change could be said to be limited to the change in temperature of the Earth, but a minute change in temperature range could bring the drastic change that we have faced and have been facing. We often read the news about the Amazon rainforest burning awfully and watch videos on social media. Aren't we already familiar with the impact of the currently increasing temperature of the Earth?

The increase in temperature is the reason why sea levels are rising. Consequently, barren lands are increasing, water bodies are shrinking, and agricultural lands are decreasing.

The question here is, why is the temperature increasing? The answer is simple, it's natural, but the speed at which it is increasing is alarming. It is rising at a fast rate because of the Greenhouse effect.

All About Greenhouse Effect

The world was pretty simple during the ice age; the temperature was changing at that time, too. That's how we got the Sahara Desert — the place was once a grassland, but the change in temperature with time turned it into a desert centuries ago. However, things changed when we learned to make tools and machines during the industrial era. We got machines and production of products at large numbers at the expense of oil and fuel, which we burned.

The smoke of those oils and fuels was collected on the Earth, either on the ground or in the air. They trap the sunlight when the rays strike them, not letting them pass through them and reach everywhere. The accumulation of hot sunlight in them turns those balls of smoke lying and dawdling on the Earth into hot balls, and the assimilation of those balls has been making our Earth hotter and hotter.

During the pre-industrial era, the carbon dioxide (CO_2) levels were 260 to 300 ppm (parts per million), but the development of industries increased to more than 300 ppm. Since then, it kept on increasing.

During the 1960s, the levels were close to 320 ppm, which reached 334 ppm in late 1974. By 1990, the level increased to 353 ppm; in early 2005, carbon dioxide levels were near 400 ppm, standing at 380 ppm.

Ten years later, in 2015, we reached 400 ppm, and currently, the carbon dioxide levels are at 420 ppm, as per the latest calculations and measurements of NASA Climate.

Methane and Climate Change

We all love to have beef burgers and chicken-filled pizzas and wraps; our parties are incomplete without pork-made meals. All our meat contributes to global warming because their feces have methane — 30% responsible for the current rise in temperature — the root of the problem we got because of the greenhouse effect.

40% of that 30% of the emission of methane is because of natural resources, but for the remaining ones, we, humans, should be blamed. After all, our needs and wants — thanks to the advertising world for making us hungrier for those things we really don't need — are fulfilled at the expense of these animals and the machines that result in methane.

Since the industrial era, methane levels have been increasing; in 1990, they were at 1700 ppb. While in 2000, methane levels increased to 1750 ppb, and 1800 ppb in 2010. In 2020, the levels increased to more than 1850 ppb, and currently, they crossed 1900 ppb.

Aren't these numbers shocking you, leaving you with popped-out eyes with a mind thinking about what we could do? The same happened when the news about floods and fire reached my ears. All I could think was, *"We need change!"*

The question of what change we could bring made me study and read a lot about climate from different books and blogs, letting me build a thorough understanding of our climate and how our world works. That knowledge helped me find the cheapest and most effective solution, which constituents the main purpose of writing this book.

The purpose of filling pages on climate change is simple, to tell everyone, from common men to large organizations, that we still have solutions if we look around the world and build understanding about the Earth. This book will help you understand thoroughly how the Earth works.

By the end of the book, the solution will be discussed with a detailed explanation of how to implement it to reduce the temperature and bring water to the deserts by using the bodies we already have.

Who Am I?

I am not a science geek or a qualified professional. I am a person like you who reads a lot and work more than required on their questions to find the answers. Science never demands you to have degrees but questions only; that's what I believe, and that's what helps me come up with the solution. I am from a humble background. Since childhood, I have seen how our planet is becoming terrible because of increasing global warming.

With the thought that we all are connected in a beautiful chain, I want to play my part and improve this world. After all, this Earth is no less than a home for us, and we all have a responsibility to make it a better place for ourselves and for the people who will come after us.

This solution could bring the change we need. The water in deserts and global temperature reduction can happen when we support the idea and encourage the world's biggest organizations to accept them and work on it.

Our Earth's climate, directly and indirectly, affects everyone's life. Therefore, a combined effort is required, and this book is the first step to bringing the idea into the world so that we all can learn how moving a little amount of water from the water bodies to the barren lands brings change.

Chapter Two — What is climate change?

Climatologists depend on different man-made historical models to predict the region's future climate. According to their models, displacement is likelier to increase by 60% due to the current awful climate change, resulting in an increment in sea levels, earthquakes, and droughts — the biggest reason for the displacement. We have the fine example of Syria, where agriculturalists had to leave their place in 2005 because of food and water insecurity that affected their land and work.

Climate-induced displacement is predicted as the biggest cause of problems in the near future. According to the recent IPCC report, researchers are working to ensure that global warming stays under 1.5°C. The question arises, *"How is it possible when our dependence on machine-made products is only increasing with time?"*

Before we answer this question, it is the necessity of this decade because the same report warns of the danger each region could face if the global temperature keeps rising. The report says that if the temperature increases more than 1.5°C, there will be:

- Extreme rainfall in Europe and the UK, which would cause floods.
- Heat waves and drought in the Middle East.

- The disappearance of islands in the Pacific Islands due to rising sea levels.
- Food and water insecurity in Africa.
- Drought in the US.
- Heat waves in Australia, which may cause wildfire and climate-induced death.

Climate Change and South Asia

South Asia, the developing region already hotter than other regions, is living and adjusting to a new-normal climate that involves heat waves and unbearable summer days in which the highest temperature is more than 40 degrees.

Unlike the Western-developed states that can use numerous resources to overcome the problems they would face, South Asia comprises poor states. Therefore, the population is likelier to look for means to displace to better places. That's why there is a new undefined word in climate change, as discussed above, climate-induced displacement.

According to the speculations, 20 million are likelier to be displaced in the next 50 years because of the rising sea levels and the new normal climate of South Asia — the most vulnerable region due to climate change.

The example of the unforgettable Kerala downpour in 2018 can explain the number of people likelier to be displaced because of the new climate. The terrible rainfall displaced 1.4 million people. According to Raya Muttarak's research paper, "Rainfall has increased 40% more than the place usually has."

Due to heavy rain in 2018, water came out of the reservoirs and dams, resulting in floods that awfully affected children and mothers because of climate-induced famine. The families suffered because of the rising cases of dengue fever, leptospirosis, acute diarrhea, and malaria. The short-termed waterborne diseases made their lives risky.

The recent flood in Pakistan alarmed everyone around the world. The humanitarian crisis in the state resulted in the displacement of more than 8 million people. Out of those, 1.8 million flood survivors still live in stagnant places. The floods affected 15% of the population, which make up 33 million people, and the damage was recorded in livestock, agriculture, transport, and housing sector. The province of Sindh was among the most affected areas where poverty increased by 5.9%, as 1.9 million went below the poverty line.

Hence, there is a dire need to establish a climate body in South Asia that drafts plans and brings them into an application that involves the construction of dams and plantations to reduce the greenhouse effect to reduce climate-induced rainfall.

Climate Change and Rainfall

The connection between climate change, global warming, and rainfall can be understood by boiling water in a saucepan. What happens when you move the knobs to a higher temperature? As more heat is produced, a greater amount of water is evaporated and collected on the surface of the lid.

The same is happening with our Earth today!

Greenhouse gases trap more heat in the Earth's atmosphere, causing average temperatures to rise all over the world. As hot air has lower density and more volume than cold air, it absorbs more evaporated water molecules and forms large clouds.

Due to the rising sea level, the process of evaporation also increases. The clouds collect water till their full capacity and get heavy, leading to rainfall in the region. Since more water is being evaporated because of the hot climate, the rainfall has been increasing.

From 1901 to 2018, there was an increase in sea levels by 20 centimeters because of the melting of glaciers and snow. As per studies, the Artic region is 65% more reduced as compared to how it was in 1975.

When the glaciers melt, their water gets mixed with fresh water, so the sea level rises, allowing a greater amount of water to evaporate and causing rainfall. This is the major reason regions such as the UK, Europe, and Asia suffer from worse rainfall that causes floods and displacement.

Climate Change and Drought

Drought is defined as the decrement in moisture that worsens agricultural production and the socioeconomic situation of people living in that region. People may have to look for other means to get water in extreme conditions.

The US has a history of facing drought for the past 18 years, resulting in a loss of around $7 billion. The impact of drought can be understood from the cases of forest fires, whose frequency has increased with time.

The western USA has been facing immense drought since the mid of 20th century, especially in California. The state is known to go through a megadrought from 2011 to 2018. According to the US Drought Monitor, exceptional drought is experienced in 32% of the western USA, affecting five states, including New Mexico, Texas, Utah, Nevada, Oregon, and California. In 2021 the conditions improved a little, but since mid of 2022, the conditions worsened due to climate change.

How does Climate Change cause drought?

As discussed, the rising temperature increases water evaporation from oceans and grounds, leading to drought. Grounds act like a sponge, absorbing everything on their surface. However, when their surface contracts due to heat, they will give up everything they absorbed. That's how the lands lose water. The warm temperature causes low precipitation and abnormal lands and water bodies drying.

The shrinkage of Las Vegas Lake is the ideal example of the connection between warm temperatures and drought.

Although the US, on paper, has come out of the longest drought that lasted for seven years, it seems that its western region will go back into the same phase as the temperature of the country has increased by 1.2°C since the early 2000s. As a result, the government is taking steps to overcome the problems they are about to face soon.

In 2021, the Interagency Drought Relief Working Group was launched to determine the financial and technical requirements to develop preventive measures. Besides, to resist drought, Bipartisan Infrastructure Law is developed to provide around $8 billion for the development of projects and the provision of clean water over the period of five years. The government is affirmed to improve the water delivery system through this money. For Western drought, $4.6 billion will be invested separately.

Climate Change and Heatwaves

"The heatwave is the new normal!"

— WMO Secretary-General

How many of you have heard this news? Do you find it true?

After all, the news of the Spanish surviving at the temperature of 45.7°C and Portugal facing immense heat because of having 47°C is in front us.

Heatwave is defined as having hot weather for a long time that may cost human lives and requires people to look for different ways to keep themselves hydrated. During the heatwave, hot air sinks down, which results in more pressure on the ground. Due to this, the air comes near the ground and becomes compressed.

Europe remained affected by the persistent heatwaves in 2022 the most, from June to August, which caused the death of 20,000 people. In May 2022, the temperatures in European countries rose for the first time since 1900. In the beginning, France suffered alone, but then Spain and Portugal also reported rising temperatures. In the same month, a heat burst occurred in France and Portugal.

In the current year, in 2023, the heatwave was reported for four days in Spain, where the temperature was more than 40°C. Due to climate change, the rainfall also decreased by 23%.

The Climate Body has devised a solution to overcome and decrease heat waves. One of them is to plant trees on streets in the city. Besides, Myrivili suggested building city forests to decrease the temperature. The UN is also focused on altering urban landscapes to reduce energy consumption and building spaces for vegetation.

Instead of applying or going for a solution that involves a lot of money, the solution to heatwaves resides in tree plantations. A small garden or trees in every street can minimize the chances of facing heat waves.

Key Takeaways

- Climate change is real, affecting almost every part of the world and bringing drastic change that we could not tolerate for a long time.

- The Climate Body of the UN has redesigned a solution that ensures the global temperature won't rise more than 1.5°C.

- According to the reports by Climate Body, climate change causes droughts, heat waves, rainfall, food insecurity, and storms.

- South Asia is the most vulnerable to climate change because of its location and economic condition. The recent floods in India and Pakistan are fine proof of it. The downpour in the two states caused awful floods that displaced millions of people and increased poverty.

- The cases explained the connection between climate change and rainfall pretty easily. Due to increased temperature, the hot air absorbs more water from the environment. Therefore, there is so much rain in the countries that the water comes out of the reservoir and causes floods.

- In America and Africa, climate-induced drought is making lives miserable. Due to warmer temperatures, more water is evaporated from the grounds and oceans, which causes humidity and drought.

- Heatwave is the biggest problem caused by climate change in which the city or a country reports warm temperature for a long time. It happens because hot air sinks down, due to which more pressure is felt on the ground. Since the last year, European countries have reported heatwaves, surpassing 40°C several times.

- Due to the current situation, it is important to take preventive measures to save the Earth from the dangers of climate change. UN suggested plantation as the cheapest and most effective means to overcome heat waves. Besides, building city forests and building spaces for vegetation could reduce the temperature.

Chapter Three — The Problem with Climate Change

Climate change is an issue that has become increasingly prominent in our global discourse as its impacts on our planet and society are becoming evident with each passing day. It is a topic that sparks discussions, debates, and concerns among individuals from all walks of life. As we delve into this complex and pressing matter, it becomes clear that significant problems associated with climate change require urgent attention.

One of the foremost issues is the increase in global temperatures. Scientific evidence overwhelmingly indicates that human activities, particularly burning fossil fuels, have rapidly increased greenhouse gas emissions, trapping heat within the Earth's atmosphere. This has resulted in rising temperatures which have devastating consequences on our environment. The melting of polar ice caps, the loss of biodiversity, and the occurrence of extreme weather events are just a few examples of the far-reaching impacts of global warming.

Another major concern relates to the rising sea levels. As temperatures soar, ice sheets and glaciers continue to melt, contributing to the gradual rise in sea levels worldwide. This poses a significant threat to coastal communities and low-lying areas, increasing the risk of flooding and displacement of populations. Small island nations, in particular, are at great risk of losing their homes and cultural heritage due to encroaching waters.

Furthermore, climate change exacerbates environmental degradation and threatens ecosystems. Deforestation, habitat destruction, and pollution further intensify the damage caused by global warming. These environmental challenges not only impact the health of our planet but also disrupt delicate ecosystems that support diverse species of plants and animals. The loss of biodiversity jeopardizes the resilience and stability of ecosystems, making them more susceptible to collapse.

At the same time, it is equally important to discuss climate change's social and economic impact. Vulnerable communities, including those in poverty, marginalized groups, and developing nations, experience disproportionate effects. Extreme weather events, droughts, and food scarcity are more likely to impact those already disadvantaged, exacerbating social inequalities and increasing social tensions. Moreover, the economic costs of climate change, including damage to infrastructure, loss of livelihoods, and increased healthcare expenses, pose significant burdens on societies around the world.

To address these problems, international cooperation and collective action are paramount.

Governments, businesses, communities, and individuals all have a role to play in mitigating climate change and adapting to its impacts. Transitioning to renewable energy sources, implementing sustainable agricultural practices, and promoting conservation efforts are crucial steps in combating climate change.

Additionally, investing in research and innovation to develop clean technologies and supporting vulnerable communities in adapting to the changing climate are essential components of an effective response.

Role of the Sun and Atmosphere

The sun, our mighty celestial neighbor, plays a crucial role in sustaining life on Earth. Its radiating energy provides warmth and light, nurturing the planet and supporting diverse ecosystems.

However, in recent years, there has been growing concern about the increasing frequency and intensity of heat waves, leading to discussions about the sun's influence and the mechanisms that keep the Earth's surface warm while the atmosphere shields and protects us.

At its core, the sun releases an enormous amount of energy in the form of electromagnetic radiation. This energy travels through space and reaches Earth in the form of sunlight. When sunlight encounters the Earth's atmosphere, a portion of it is reflected back into space, while the remaining energy passes through and interacts with the planet's surface.

The key to understanding global warming lies in the concept of the greenhouse effect. The Earth's surface absorbs a significant amount of the sun's energy, converting it into heat. This heat is then radiated back into the atmosphere as infrared radiation. Greenhouse gases, such as carbon dioxide (CO_2), methane (CH_4), and water vapors, act as natural insulators, trapping a portion of this infrared radiation and preventing it from escaping into space. This process keeps the Earth's surface warmer than it would be otherwise.

The atmosphere plays a vital role in regulating heat distribution across the planet. As sunlight passes through the atmosphere, it undergoes various interactions. Some of the energy is absorbed into the atmosphere, particularly by the ozone layer, which protects us from harmful ultraviolet (UV) radiation. The remaining energy reaches the Earth's surface, where it warms the land, oceans, and vegetation.

The warmth of the Earth's surface is further maintained through processes like conduction, convection, and latent heat transfer.

Conduction occurs when heat is transferred through direct contact between materials, for example, heat transfer from the ground to your bare feet on a sunny day. Convection involves the movement of heat through air or water circulation, like how warm air rises, and cool air descends. Latent heat transfer refers to the absorption or release of heat energy during the phase changes of water, such as evaporation and condensation.

While the sun's rays provide the primary source of heat, the atmosphere acts as a protective shield for the Earth. It absorbs harmful ultraviolet radiation, preventing it from reaching the surface and shielding us from its detrimental effects. The atmosphere also regulates temperature variations, distributing heat across the planet through weather patterns and ocean currents.

However, it is essential to note that human activities, particularly burning fossil fuels and deforestation, have increased greenhouse gas concentrations in the atmosphere. This human-induced enhancement of the greenhouse effect also contributes to a rise in global temperatures, leading to more frequent and intense heat waves.

Increase in Human Population

The relationship between human population growth and climate change is complex and multifaceted. While population growth is not the sole cause of climate change, it is a significant factor that contributes to the problem. Some key points to consider that contribute to climate change are listed below.

- **Emissions and Resource Consumption**: As the global population increases, the demand for energy, food, water, and other resources also increase. The production and consumption of these resources often involve burning fossil fuels, deforestation, and other activities that release greenhouse gases (GHGs) into the atmosphere, leading to climate change.

- **Land Use Change**: The expansion of human settlements and infrastructure often leads to deforestation and the conversion of natural habitats, such as forests and wetlands, into agricultural land or urban areas. This loss of natural ecosystems reduces the Earth's capacity to absorb carbon dioxide and disrupts natural carbon cycles.

- **Urbanization**: Rapid urbanization is occurring in many parts of the world, with people moving from rural areas to cities. Urban areas tend to have higher energy demands, increased transportation needs, and concentrated industrial activities, all of which contribute to higher carbon emissions.

- **Agricultural Practices**: As the population grows, more land is needed for agriculture to feed the expanding human population. Large-scale agriculture, particularly livestock farming, is a significant source of GHG emissions, especially methane from livestock and nitrous oxide from fertilizers.
- **Vulnerability and Adaptation**: Rising sea levels, extreme weather events, and changing rainfall patterns are among the climate change effects that can disproportionately affect densely populated regions. High population density can increase vulnerability to climate-related risks and strain resources and infrastructure during and after such events.

It's important to note that population growth alone is not solely responsible for climate change. Technological advancements, economic systems, consumption patterns, and energy sources also play crucial roles. Addressing climate change requires a comprehensive approach that considers population dynamics, sustainable development, energy transition, resource efficiency, and adaptation strategies.

What are the solutions to climate change?

Addressing climate change requires a combination of mitigation and adaptation strategies. Here are some proposed solutions that can help mitigate and adapt to climate change:

- **Transition to Renewable Energy**: Shifting from fossil fuels to renewable energy sources such as solar, wind, hydro, and geothermal power can significantly reduce greenhouse gas emissions. Investing in renewable energy infrastructure, promoting research and development, and implementing supportive policies and incentives are crucial steps in this transition.

- **Energy Efficiency**: Improving energy efficiency in buildings, transportation, and industrial processes can reduce energy consumption and lower emissions. This can be achieved through energy-efficient technologies, building insulation, efficient appliances, and sustainable transportation systems such as electric vehicles.

- **Sustainable Land Use and Forest Conservation**: Protecting and restoring forests and adopting sustainable land management practices can help sequester carbon dioxide and preserve biodiversity. Reducing deforestation, promoting afforestation and reforestation, and implementing sustainable agriculture techniques can contribute to carbon sequestration and mitigate climate change.

- **Low-Carbon Transportation**: Encouraging the use of public transportation, cycling, and walking, as well as transitioning to electric vehicles, can reduce emissions from the transportation sector. It is also essential to invest in efficient and accessible public transportation systems and support the development of electric vehicle infrastructure.

- **Circular Economy and Sustainable Consumption:** Transitioning to a circular economy, where resources are used efficiently, waste is minimized, and materials are recycled or repurposed, can reduce the environmental impact of production and consumption. Promoting sustainable consumption patterns, reducing food waste, and implementing recycling and waste management strategies are important steps.

- **Climate Policy and International Cooperation**: Implementing comprehensive climate policies, such as carbon pricing mechanisms, emissions trading systems, and regulatory frameworks, can create incentives for emissions reductions. International cooperation and agreements, like the Paris Agreement, are crucial for global efforts to combat climate change.

- **Adaptation and Resilience**: Investing in climate change adaptation measures is essential to reduce vulnerability and build resilience in communities and ecosystems. This includes improving infrastructure, developing early warning systems, protecting coastal areas, and implementing water management strategies to cope with changing climate conditions.

- **Public Awareness and Education**: Increasing public awareness about climate change and its impacts is crucial for fostering collective action. Education and communication campaigns can help promote sustainable behaviors, encourage community engagement, and support adopting climate-friendly practices.

What is the significance of these solutions?

Finding solutions for climate change is crucial for our planet's and future generations' long-term sustainability and well-being. The urgency of addressing climate change arises from its far-reaching impacts on multiple fronts.

First and foremost, climate change has severe environmental consequences. Rising global temperatures, melting glaciers, and sea-level rise pose significant threats to ecosystems and biodiversity. Habitats are being disrupted, leading to the loss of plant and animal species, and ecosystems are becoming imbalanced. By finding solutions, we can mitigate these impacts and safeguard the Earth's natural resources, ensuring their preservation for future generations.

Moreover, climate change directly affects human lives and livelihoods. Extreme weather events such as hurricanes, droughts, and floods are becoming more frequent and intense, resulting in the displacement of communities, destruction of infrastructure, and loss of lives. Health risks are amplified, with heatwaves, the spread of vector-borne diseases, and worsened air pollution impacting human well-being. Finding solutions for climate change is essential to protect vulnerable populations, improve public health, and enhance the overall quality of life.

Economically, climate change poses significant risks. Extreme weather events and natural disasters disrupt agricultural production, leading to food shortages and price volatility. Coastal areas face increased vulnerability due to rising sea levels, impacting industries such as tourism and fisheries. Moreover, climate change poses financial risks, potentially damaging property, infrastructure, and businesses.

Addressing climate change and implementing sustainable practices can foster economic stability, promote innovation, and create green jobs in renewable energy and other low-carbon sectors.

Furthermore, climate change is an issue of social justice. Vulnerable communities, particularly in developing countries, often bear the brunt of climate impacts, despite contributing the least to greenhouse gas emissions. Finding solutions involves addressing social inequalities and ensuring that climate policies prioritize the needs of marginalized groups, promoting equity and climate justice.

Lastly, the global nature of climate change necessitates international cooperation and collaboration. Finding solutions requires collective action, with governments, businesses, communities, and individuals working together to reduce emissions, transition to sustainable practices, and support climate resilience. By engaging in collaborative efforts, we can harness collective knowledge and resources to achieve meaningful and effective solutions on a global scale.

Chapter Four — New Solution

Overcoming the issue of climate change requires a collaborative effort from all the stakeholders, including the general public, business tycoons, environmentalists, and renowned organizations, to devise an effective solution. For years, companies and organizations have suggested reducing the use of fossils as a source of energy and taking steps to protect forests. The question arises, is it appropriate in this age when we all rely on man-made and machine-made products in our daily lives?

The answer is **NO!**

Firstly, we have become dependent on these products. Secondly, we need a solution that brings instant change as we can no longer afford to live on a planet where hot weather and heat waves affect our lifestyles to the core.

The issue of climate change interests me the most, leading me to study more about it, aiming to find a solution. Reading books and blogs, along with listening to podcasts and movies, boggle me with one question, what could we do to improve the living conditions on our planet?

About 70% of the Earth's surface is covered with water, out of which 96.6% is in oceans, and the remaining 2.5% is drinkable. As I studied about it, I was curious to know if we could use all of the water we already have on Earth.

Reading about the issues led me to the solution of moving water to less green areas, deserts, or mountains.

Moving Water Inland

As per the technique I devised after a thorough reading, the organizations and government have to work with the environmentalists to transfer 10 to 20% of the water from the rivers and oceans to the barren lands.

Each country can use this technique as per their need to overcome the climate and water issues in the required areas and cities.

The technique has been used in the past in America. In the 1930s, Tennessee Valley Authority established that move water into the Tennessee River Valley with the help of power plants, dams, and reservoirs to overcome drought and flooding. The aim of providing moving water in the valley is to irrigate the land, continue using hydroelectric power, and facilitate the people with the availability of drinking water.

California State Water Project is another example of moving water inland, where the system of canals and pipelines was installed during the 1930s in the Sierra Nevada Mountains for the transportation of water to Southern California to overcome drought in the area. The technique helped in the conduction of irrigation methods and the availability of drinkable water.

Benefits of moving water Inland

Moving water inland is a known technique that can reduce the temperature of the geographical location where it is practiced too little. There are several advantages to it.

Some of them are:

Sea level:

Many oceans and rivers hold more water than their potential, leading to maximum chances of having a flood. Moving water from those rivers to deserts will help control the sea level. Environmentalists usually build dams and reservoirs to move water inland, aiming to reduce the chances of water flowing out on the land from rivers and oceans.

Drought

Installing pipelines and canals supplements the process of moving water from water bodies to drought-affected areas.

Wildfires

By building reservoirs and lakes, water is moved inland to places likely to be affected by wildfire, aiming to provide water to firefighters to ensure safety.

Earth temperature

Moving a small percentage of water from water bodies to barren lands reduce the volume of water available for evaporation, leading to cooler temperatures. Eventually, the technique will lessen the greenhouse effect.

How can water be moved to Barren Lands from oceans and rivers?

Usually, as discussed above, pipelines and canal systems are built and installed to transport water from rivers and oceans to far-away cities and drought-affected areas. Besides, the cities and countries have large pumps installed underground to transport water from the water bodies to the cities. With the growing use of technology, environmentalists use turbines and solar-powered pumps to move water inland.

Use of turbine

The turbine is majorly connected to power pumps to move water from water bodies to irrigation canals for agricultural purposes.

Secondly, they are used to generate electricity for the power pumps to move water in the lands in a sustainable manner with minimum to no need for fossils.

Use of solar-based water pumps

Solar-based water pumps are used to move desalinated water from oceans to nearby areas for drinking. In the beginning, the machine removes salt from the water and then transports it to the nearby areas for irrigation and consumption. Companies and scientists are looking for ways to use it to move water to drought-stricken areas.

Moving water inland and greenery

Moving water inland causes the hydration of the land, which eventually improves plantation and soil quality in most cases. In the case of the California State Water Project, the irrigation of millions of acres of land in the state results in the growth of millions of trees. Similarly, trees are found growing in Tennessee Valley because of the Tennessee Valley Authority due to the irrigation of a large number of lands.

Plant growth:

Moving water from oceans and rivers to land areas reduces dehydration and humidity, which fosters the environment that supplements the growth of plants.

Improved soil quality

Movement of water to the land areas results in the absorption of the water on the ground, which works as a medium for the nutrients and organic matter to get mixed, maximizing the chances of having greenery in the area.

Reduced erosion

Transportation of water to land areas washes away the loose soil and sediments that eventually protect plants and soil from damage.

Moving water inland and rainfall

Using pumps for the transportation of water to land areas improves the weather cycle, which results in rainfall. Yet, there are the following reasons why moving water inland causes rainfall. The example of Aswan High Dam is in front of us, whose establishment to move water inland increased rainfall in Egypt.

Evaporation

Moving water inland causes more evaporation of the water transported to the specific land, which results in the condensation of the droplets into clouds. The clouds burst once they are collected in big amounts, resulting in rainfalls.

Wind patterns

The betterment in weather due to the transportation of water to the land areas results in changes in wind patterns, bringing more moisture. Therefore, such lands are more likely to have rainfall than lands where water is not transported.

Plantation

Moving water inland improves plantation, leading to cool weather that promotes rainfall in the long term.

The role of organizations in moving water inland

Working on climate is not the task of one organization as it involves millions of investments, the effort of researchers, and a team of laborers to turn the idea into reality with the motive of protecting the environment. Based on the data received from scientists and reporters, numerous organizations and scientists currently work under one umbrella to make the Earth a better place. United Nations, Climate Action Network (CAN), Environmental Defense Fund (EDF), Natural Resources Defense Council (NRDC), and World Wildlife Fund (WWF) are a few of the organizations devising solutions and policies to improve the climate.

Besides, a team of people in different areas under different brands and NGOs raises awareness of saving the Earth, such as 350.org, Climate Action Now, Climate Cardinals, and Climate Collaborative.

However, bringing change is only possible when the world's big companies, like Apple, Google, and Microsoft, will take their role seriously in raising their voice about climate change.

After all, they are the major contributors to climate change as they consume a billion kilowatts of electricity. Working with known climate organizations will not only successfully implement effective solutions but help people understand the need to save the climate. The companies can use their monetary power to execute the strategies, their team to provide guidance, and help the organizations devise better plans.

Moreover, the data providers can collaborate with the organizations to supplement their research work. Most importantly, brands can play a keen role in raising awareness and advocating for policy change.

Chapter Five — Execution

The ideating process is the first step toward bringing change, but the execution phase defines one's consistency toward their goals. For us and the organizations, making policies that promote a healthy climate and better environment is easy because it does not involve physical labor.

Implementing the technique I devised for moving water inland is possible, but in order to execute globally, there is a need to have a working map or action plan to apply this process in every continent and country with time while giving freedom to the state to use the technique where required.

Below is the list of eight methods to execute the process of moving water inland in the world:

Method 1: Individual countries

The first method involves encouraging all countries to transport water from their water bodies to the required areas. The climate organizations of their state must provide the government officials guidelines based on their geography to move the water.

Method 2: Installation of Pipelines

The organizations can first focus on lakes and rivers whose water level is the same as the land's to minimize the risk of floods. The organizations can install pipelines to build canals for water transportation, or they can simply use land pipes for this purpose.

Method 3: Generation of Electricity

In this technique, organizations can use low-leveled water bodies to generate electricity in the required areas. The technicians can install water pumps that run on wind, solar, or any fuel to produce free electricity.

Method 4: Installation of Tunnels

This trick focuses on installing tunnels for water transportation to deserts, mountains, lakes, and other areas.

Method 5: Network of Pipes

Organizations can also install a long network of pipes and pressure pumps to move water into the land areas, especially mountains.

Method 6: The Egyptian Model

This method is effective for countries where water from lakes and rivers empties into the sea or ocean. In order to keep water in the lakes, this method focuses on building dams in front of that lake or river from where the water can be moved to other sources.

Egypt is known for facing the problem as its River Nile mainly empties into the Mediterranean Sea. Building dams can save the water from moving into other water bodies. Yet, the constructors are required to build a dam with a reasonable height that can stop the movement of water and transfer it back to the canals to be used. Implementing this method years ago could have created a small permanent river parallel to the Nile in Egypt.

Method 7: Network of Lakes

Implementing the methods mentioned above can save a lot of drinkable water, which we, in turn, can be utilized by building a network of lakes and reservoirs.

Method 8: Solar Panels

This method involves using solar panels to cover the networks of canals and lakes. Solar panels allow us to use the water for drinking, agriculture, personal use, and to generate electricity.

Government officials can collaborate with the climate organizations of their state to understand the geography and climate before deciding the method they are going to apply.

Why apply these methods?

Implementing these methods demands huge investments; therefore, every nation needs to make a wise decision to minimize the loss. Each of these methods is beneficial, but it is important to ensure that the geographical location of the country is suitable for it or not. Some of the advantages of the methods mentioned above are:

- Method two lowers the sea and oceans level to minimize the chances of flood and the disappearance of the cities.

- Transportation of water to lands will cause more rainfall in those areas where water is moved. Eventually, there will be plantations, and new woods will grow there.

- The implementation of these methods will help us control climate.

- Reduction in the temperature of every state due to moving water inland will eventually reduce the temperature of the globe and the cases of heatwaves.

- Applying these methods will reduce the thinning of ice in the mountains.
- Moving water to different land areas from rivers and lakes will create more communities that eventually create more employment opportunities.
- There will be more woody areas with the implementation of these methods.
- Transportation of water will improve agriculture and promote the growth of more crops.
- More lakes can be created as natural resources, allowing the fishing industry to thrive.
- This will provide an opportunity to build more resorts in the area.
- There will be a reduction in drought seasons, floods, and storms because of moving water to land areas.
- Moving water inland will reduce wildfire and shortage of food supply.
- Water bodies will become accessible to a large population in every country.

Transportation of water from different sources to land areas is beneficial at the state and global levels. It reduces the chances of drought and the number of barren lands, eventually promoting plantation and irrigation that guarantees the betterment of human life. States can carry out the process of moving water inland in different techniques and methods that suit their topographical conditions to overcome the challenges posed by climate change.

Chapter Six — Conclusion

Climate change is a global issue, impacting human life and our environment in a myriad of ways. In light of growing cases of heatwaves, floods, storms, and earthquakes, it is also the major cause of several deaths worldwide.

According to scientists, there are two major causes of the worse changes in the climate:

- Rising temperatures, and
- Human activities.

Temperature and Climate Change

Scientists confirmed with the data they collected through tools and utter observation that the sun is becoming hotter, giving more radiation which is natural. However, the speed at which the temperature is rising is alarming because it is making the Earth an unbearable place to live.

Due to the greenhouse effect, the atmosphere cannot perform its function of working as a blanket over the land. It remains warm, so the Earth is pressured, eventually making us feel hot.

Human Activities

The fact that we have become habitual of machine-made products for all purposes is the reason why greenhouse effects take a toll on climate change, causing heatwaves and wildfires around the world. The tremendous increment in human population further contributes to industrialization, which is the root of all problems.

Encouraging a common person to change their habits is next to impossible because our fast-paced lives do not allow us to perform certain tasks with our own hands. Thus, there is a need to look for other ways to improve the climate globally. Currently, the United Nations has set a few targets to address these issues and take initiatives to overcome the damage being caused due to climate change.

But the question arises, can the UN alone bring the change that we need?

The answer is **NO!**

Climate change is not an issue that can be solved in a year or by just one person, country, or organization. It requires a collective effort from all states and all people in their own way.

I am a guy from a humble background with a simple mind and education record. My interests made me study a lot about global warming and climate change, which eventually compelled me to find a solution.

Thorough reading and skimming research papers led me to find the solution that I believe can solve the major part of our problem — moving water inland. Transportation of water from the river, oceans, and lakes to barren lands is not a new method; in fact, it was used years ago, especially in the 20th century, by building dams and canal barrages to save the water and move it to the required places in the country.

This technique can still be applied in different ways to reduce the global temperature, allowing each country to move water to land areas in their way, based on their location and needs. As discussed in the previous chapter, I have devised eight methods to transport water from different sources to land areas.

The first involves giving the right to each country to use the technique as per their feasibility to cater to their needs. The second method focuses on installing pipelines to reduce the water level in the water bodies and minimize catastrophes. Besides, countries and organizations can also install water pumps in low-leveled water bodies to generate electricity in those areas where required. Moreover, tunnels can mainly be installed to transport water from lakes and rivers to deserts.

The fifth method focuses on installing a network of pumps and pipes to move water to mountainous areas. The sixth method is the Egyptian model, in which the technicians can build dams near the rivers or lakes that empties into other sources or water bodies. This method could have been used years ago in Egypt to save the River Nile. The seventh and eighth method is all about using solar panels over canals to save the water we collect from natural resources and build a network of lakes to store the water for different purposes. Transportation of water to land areas affected by drought can fulfill the requirement for water in those communities. It also promotes plantations and agriculture that eventually reduce famine and the temperature of the place. As the region's temperature cools down, it reduces the occurrence of heat waves and other catastrophes, ultimately improving human lives.

Moreover, it also helps in building new communities, which ultimately create more job opportunities. Most importantly, installing pipelines and building a network of lakes and canals can make the water more accessible to a large population of the state. We must remember that working to improve the climate is not the sole responsibility of the UN; the public, business tycoons, and large enterprises, being the major reason for global warming, should put their heart, soul, and resources into climate organizations to overcome the damaging effects of climate change on our planet.

Companies like Tesla, Amazon, Google, and others can use their capital and technical expertise to devise the solution. They also use their medium and reach to raise awareness among the general public to teach them about the harmful impact of climate change on the environment. These companies can also use their platforms and services to assist climate organizations in changing their policy to bring the idea into reality.

The purpose of writing this book is very simple. I want to tell the readers that there is a solution to climate change that is applicable and guarantees betterment for all. I used all my knowledge and work to share what I learned with you because we all deserve to live in a better world.

Through this book, I want to convey my idea to the leaders of the world and influencers who have the power to take the initiative and raise awareness on a larger scale. I have attached a letter that I would like to send to all big giants and organizations of the world as a request to play their part in this noble cause.

This book will not bring change overnight, but I hope that it creates awareness among people to realize what we need right now. This realization will help me reach the people who have the power to devise policies and bring change.

An important message about my new Climate change solution.

Messages sent on June – August 2023

Dear Countries, World leaders, UN secretary-general, UN environment and climate organizations, research centers, and Universities.

Will you be part of my efforts to implement the new climate solution all over the World?

I hope that you join the research of my new and easy climate changes solution:

(Moving Sea Water inland to Control Sea level, drought, wildfires, and Earth's temperature +)

#AquaShift

In the next few days, we hope to start our research in many countries that will focus on two major goals after moving Sea and Ocean Water to areas on our planet, especially deserts, uninhabited areas, and high-temperature spots, where it never rained before:

1. Will that lower the temperature in the areas where we moved the water into them?

2. Will we see some rain in those areas?

Your support is essential to study, research, and apply this solution.

The plan is to start implementing this solution in many areas in different countries as soon as possible and share the results with the whole world.

We hope to form a team of experts from the UN, many countries, research centers, and universities. Any support will be highly appreciated as we need volunteers and experts from all over the world.

The world is waiting for your help and support to start applying this solution.

Please review all details about my solution in the attached book (Before it's too late, Climate), which I published on June 24, 2023, on Amazon/ Kindle, Barnes &Noble, and other platforms all over the World.

A copy of the same letter sent to the UN is published on pages 49 – 50 of my book.

Regards,

Dean Khater

Chapter Seven — Summary

The idea, the solution is simple. Most countries can implement it in just a few days.

(Moving Sea Water inland to Control Sea level, drought, wildfires, and Earth's temperature +)

#AquaShift

A Game-changing solution and A revolutionary solution for Climate change

Using wind turbines and solar-based water pumps to move water from oceans and seas to land. This can prove to be a simple solution. It can become applicable at a very low cost and is guaranteed to solve many of climate change's problems.

Harnessing renewable energy, these technologies could potentially alleviate water scarcity, benefiting drought-prone regions. Solar pumps and wind turbines operate sustainably, reducing carbon emissions. Moreover, once desalinated, the moved ocean water can replenish, depleting freshwater resources, supporting agriculture and human consumption. However, this plan requires careful evaluation of ecological impacts and technical feasibility for successful implementation.

This idea can be implemented immediately and could potentially be applied in nearly every country. If it proves ineffective, we can simply halt the movement of water from the seas and oceans inland. The water would evaporate in a matter of days. Time is of the essence, and the world should begin applying this solution now. There's no harm in attempting every potential solution.

We are already aware of the existing problem, and yet, the worst is still to come.

The beauty of this approach is its reversibility and low risk. With climate change threatening our future, such innovative, eco-friendly solutions are essential. We must remember every small step counts in our global fight against this crisis.

Countries, regardless of their geographical location or economic status, could consider this solution. While it may not completely eradicate the problem, it could help alleviate its severity, buying us time to find more comprehensive solutions.

Implementing the new solution today, World will solve most of climate change's problems in 2 weeks.

1- Lower Seas and Oceans levels to the safest possible levels to avoid the disappearance of many cities.

   By strategically reducing sea and ocean levels, we could safeguard numerous cities currently threatened by rising water levels.

   This plan could serve as a vital buffer against the devastating impacts of climate change, particularly in coastal areas.

2- Once we have more water-covered areas, eventually, those areas will have good amounts of rain to start a new life, new woods, and areas ready to be planted with all kinds of crops and plants to feed millions.

With increased water coverage, rainfall would naturally follow, stimulating the growth of new ecosystems.
These areas could transform into lush woodlands or arable land, ready to cultivate a variety of crops and plants, thereby sustaining and nourishing millions of people.

3- We will control the climate forever.

4- The whole planet's temperature will be dramatically lower than it is now. No more brutal heatwaves in many countries mean fewer health problems.

A significant drop in global temperatures would alleviate the current rise in heat waves, contributing to a more balanced climate.

This, in turn, would reduce heat-related health issues, improving the overall quality of life and potentially lessening the burden on healthcare systems worldwide.

5- We will stop the ice melting in north and south areas on our Earth forever, or the ice on the high mountains and Antarctica too.

6- We will create many jobs for many people in the new communities that will be created by covering them with water already transferred from oceans and seas.

7- More wooded areas.

8- More agricultural areas to grow all kinds of plants, fruits, wheat, vegetables, and other kinks of plants.

9- If some areas are far or hard to reach, we will leave them as they are with water covered, which will reduce the whole global Earth's temperature and rain, where it never rained before.

10- We will make many new lakes as natural resources and natural wildlife.

11- Make some resorts in the area where they are suitable for those purposes.

12- New Lakes areas and Rivers.

13- No more frequent and intense drought.

14- No more heavy storms.

15- No more melting glaciers and warming oceans

16- Less global warming.

17- Less heavy floods.

18- No shortage of water for daily usage and irrigation.

19- No drought and water shortage for drinking and irrigation.

20- No interruption in food supplies.

21- Generate green, safe, and free electricity.

22- No more wildfires in many high-heated areas on our planet.

23- We will have less deserts and less mountains.

24- New fishing areas to supply cheap seafood.

25- Many tourist and resort areas will be created.

26- With this solution, all countries will have new seas, shores, ports, lakes, and rivers.

We must know and always remember our World Population.

Do we have enough food and water?

For all humanity? The answer is no, but the new solution will make Earth greener to grow more crops.

World population record:

Year	World Population
2020	7,794,798,739
2019	7,713,468,100
2018	7,631,091,040
2017	7,547,858,925
2016	7,464,022,049
2015	7,379,797,139
2014	7,295,290,765
2013	7,210,581,976
2012	7,125,828,059
2011	7,041,194,301
2010	6,956,823,603
2009	6,872,767,093
2008	6,789,088,686
2007	6,705,946,610
2006	6,623,517,833
2005	6,541,907,027
2004	6,461,159,389
2003	6,381,185,114

2002	6,301,773,188
2001	6,222,626,606
2000	6,143,493,823
1999	6,064,239,055
1998	5,984,793,942
1997	5,905,045,788
1996	5,824,891,951
1995	5,744,212,979
1994	5,663,150,427
1993	5,581,597,546
1992	5,498,919,809
1991	5,414,289,444
1990	5,327,231,061
1989	5,237,441,558
1988	5,145,426,008
1987	5,052,522,147
1986	4,960,567,912
1985	4,870,921,740
1984	4,784,011,621
1983	4,699,569,304
1982	4,617,386,542
1981	4,536,996,762

1980	4,458,003,514
1979	4,380,506,100
1978	4,304,533,501
1977	4,229,506,060
1976	4,154,666,864
1975	4,079,480,606
1974	4,003,794,172
1973	3,927,780,238
1972	3,851,650,245
1971	3,775,759,617
1970	3,700,437,046
1969	3,625,680,627
1968	3,551,599,127
1967	3,478,769,962
1966	3,407,922,630
1965	3,339,583,597
1964	3,273,978,338
1963	3,211,001,009
1962	3,150,420,795
1961	3,091,843,507
1960	3,034,949,748
1959	2,979,576,185

1958	2,925,686,705
1957	2,873,306,090
1956	2,822,443,282
1955	2,773,019,936
1954	2,724,846,741
1953	2,677,608,960
1952	2,630,861,562
1951	2,584,034,261
1927	2,000,000,000
1700	610,000,000
1600	500,000,000
1500	450,000,000
1400	350,000,000

Climate changes news and headlines from social media and news organizations from every corner of the World:

"Have we reached a climate apocalypse"

"U.N. official Decarbonization might not happen fast enough to stop climate change."

"Sick of hearing about record heat, Scientists say those numbers paint the story of a warming world."

"Sea Ice Is Going, But When Will It Be Gone."

"Catastrophic climate 'doom loops' could start in just 15 years, a new study warns."

"Time is running out on the Climate Clock."

"Research reveals the concerning, little-known factor that makes heat waves so deadly — and why it could be getting worse."

"Antarctic has an Ozone hole the size of North America."

"Climate change is changing the ocean's color — and fast, scientists say."

"Earth is Screaming' Meteorologist Warns Amid Unprecedented Heatwave 'Need To Listen"

"The climate crisis is here."

"Wake up, World. Climate change is real."

"Climate change solutions available. Act now!"

"Climate change -Code red for humanity."

"World must wake up and act to curb climate change before it's too late."

"Before it's too late, Climate."

"What Happens If... We Actually Exceed 1.5°C In Global Warming?"

"A new dangerous, long-lasting heat wave could set dozens of heat records, even in notoriously hot places."

"Antarctic Ice Reaches Record-Smashing Low, Alarming Scientists"

"Antarctica's Doomsday Glacier is melting much faster than expected."

"Baked Alaska Climate change's extreme heat is warming the state and creating national security problems."

"Killer heatwave mapped making its way through Europe."

"Sinking cities Climate change is warping the ground our cities are built on, study says."

"Two global records in two days, the climate crisis and the warming of the North Atlantic take the planet into uncharted territory."

"The Weight of New York City: Possible Contributions to Subsidence from Anthropogenic Sources."

"Countries and Cities Could Be Underwater By 2050, or Before."

The Maldives. - Kiribati - Vanuatu.

Solomon Island – Tuvalu - Samoa –

Fiji Island - Nauru."

"Welcome to the Anthropocene, Earth's new chapter."

"Underground climate change threatened to destabilize infrastructure at large."

"MIT climate scientist urges action after hottest days on record."

"New data raises concerns over global sea level."

"a new study into how quickly ice sheets melted at the end of the last ice age is raising the alarm over how quickly sea levels could rise in today's warming world."

"UN calls for complete shutdown to fossil fuel shut down"

"We're Running out of time. - Climate change is getting BAD."

"Climate Change Is Speeding Toward Catastrophe. The Next Decade Is Crucial, U.N. Panel Says."

"A new report says it is still possible to hold global warming to relatively safe levels, but doing so will require global cooperation, billions of dollars, and big changes."

"Scientists deliver 'final warning' on climate crisis: act now or it's too late."

"Is the World ready to solve the climate change problems?"

The following important message was sent to all Countries, World leaders, the UN secretary-general, UN Environment, and climate organizations, most of the research centers, and most of the Universities in the USA, Europe, and the rest of the World:

An important message about my new Climate changes solution

Messages sent on June – August 2023

Dear Countries, World leaders, UN secretary-general, UN environment and climate organizations, research centers, and Universities,

Will you be part of my efforts to implement the new climate solution all over the World

I hope that you join the research of my new and easy climate changes solution:

(Moving Sea Water inland to Control Sea level, drought, wildfires, and Earth's temperature +)

#AquaShift

In the next few days, we hope to start our research in many countries that will focus on two major goals after moving Sea and Ocean Water to areas on our planet, especially deserts, uninhabited areas, and high-temperature spots, where it never rained before:

1. Will that lower the temperature in the areas where we moved the water into them?
2. Will we see some rain in those areas?

Your support is essential to study, research, and apply this solution.

The plan is to start implementing this solution in many areas in different countries as soon as possible and share the results with the whole world.

We hope to form a team of experts from the UN, many countries, research centers, and universities. Any support will be highly appreciated as we need volunteers and experts from all over the world.

The world is waiting for your help and support to start applying this solution.

Please review all details about my solution in the attached book (Before it's too late, Climate), which I published on June 24, 2023, on Amazon/ Kindle, Barnes &Noble, and other platforms all over the World.

A copy of the same letter sent to the UN is published on pages 49 – 50 of my book.

Regards,

Dean Khater

I did my best to come up with new ideas and solutions. I hope this new solution will help us to stop climate change. I hope the whole World listens and tries to implement my solution.

Dean Khater

August 2023

2023 (The warmest year on record.)

Time is running out

The solution

(Moving Sea Water inland to Control Sea level, drought, wildfires, and Earth's temperature +)

#AquaShift

August 1, 2023

Message to: Secretary-General of the United Nations

Will you be part of our efforts to implement the new climate solution all over the World?

I hope that you join the research of my new and easy climate changes solution:

(Moving Sea Water inland to Control Sea level, drought, wildfires, and Earth's temperature +)

#AquaShift

Regards,

Dean Khater

Earth is waiting

The solution

(Moving Sea Water inland to Control Sea level, drought, wildfires, and Earth's temperature +)

#AquaShift

August 1, 2023

Message to: Italy

Will you be part of our efforts to implement the new climate solution all over the World?

I hope that you join the research of my new and easy climate changes solution:

(Moving Sea Water inland to Control Sea level, drought, wildfires, and Earth's temperature +)

#AquaShift

Regards,
Dean Khater

Climate changes, can we stop it, act now

The solution

(Moving Sea Water inland to Control Sea level, drought, wildfires, and Earth's temperature +)

#AquaShift

August 1, 2023

Message to: Algeria

Will you be part of our efforts to implement the new climate solution all over the World?

I hope that you join the research of my new and easy climate changes solution:

(Moving Sea Water inland to Control Sea level, drought, wildfires, and Earth's temperature +)

#AquaShift

Regards,
Dean Khater

It dosen't heart to try this solution

The solution

(Moving Sea Water inland to Control Sea level, drought, wildfires, and Earth's temperature +)

#AquaShift

August 1, 2023

Message to: France

Will you be part of our efforts to implement the new climate solution all over the World?

I hope that you join the research of my new and easy climate changes solution:

(Moving Sea Water inland to Control Sea level, drought, wildfires, and Earth's temperature +)

#AquaShift

Regards,
Dean Khater

What are you waiting for

The solution

(Moving Sea Water inland to Control Sea level, drought, wildfires, and Earth's temperature +)

#AquaShift

August 1, 2023

Message to: UNFCC

Will you be part of our efforts to implement the new climate solution all over the World?

I hope that you join the research of my new and easy climate changes solution:

(Moving Sea Water inland to Control Sea level, drought, wildfires, and Earth's temperature +)

#AquaShift

Regards,
Dean Khater

This is a uniqe solution

The solution

(Moving Sea Water inland to Control Sea level, drought, wildfires, and Earth's temperature +)

#AquaShift

August 1, 2023

Message to: MIT - USA

Will you be part of our efforts to implement the new climate solution all over the World?

I hope that you join the research of my new and easy climate changes solution:

(Moving Sea Water inland to Control Sea level, drought, wildfires, and Earth's temperature +)

#AquaShift

Regards,

Dean Khater

This is the only hope

       The solution

(Moving Sea Water inland to Control Sea level, drought, wildfires, and Earth's temperature +)

#AquaShift

August 1, 2023

Message to: The Intergovernmental Panel on Climate Change (IPCC)

Will you be part of our efforts to implement the new climate solution all over the World?

I hope that you join the research of my new and easy climate changes solution:

(Moving Sea Water inland to Control Sea level, drought, wildfires, and Earth's temperature +)

#AquaShift

Regards,

Dean Khater

No other solution is available

        The solution

(Moving Sea Water inland to Control Sea level, drought, wildfires, and Earth's temperature +)

#AquaShift

August 1, 2023

Message to: UN Environment Programme

Will you be part of our efforts to implement the new climate solution all over the World?

I hope that you join the research of my new and easy climate changes solution:

(Moving Sea Water inland to Control Sea level, drought, wildfires, and Earth's temperature +)

#AquaShift

Regards,

Dean Khater

Finding a solution is the responsabilty of all of us

The solution

(Moving Sea Water inland to Control Sea level, drought, wildfires, and Earth's temperature +)

#AquaShift

August 1, 2023

Message to: Google

Will you be part of our efforts to implement the new climate solution all over the World?

I hope that you join the research of my new and easy climate changes solution:

(Moving Sea Water inland to Control Sea level, drought, wildfires, and Earth's temperature +)

#AquaShift

Regards,

Dean Khater

Before It's Too Late, Climate

A Game-Changing Solution

Dean Khater

www.deankhater.com

August 2023

Made in the USA
Columbia, SC
24 August 2023

46740f9b-446e-403d-8dd6-69359085df4fR01